D0646916

DISCARD

5-02

Mick Manning & Brita Granström

Nature WATCH

KINGFISHER

NEW YORK

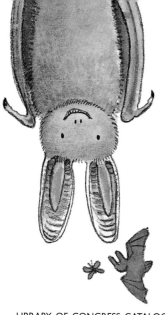

KINGFISHER
Larousse Kingfisher Chambers Inc.
95 Madison Avenue
New York, New York 10016

First published 1997
10 9 8 7 6 5 4 3 2

Copyright © Mick Manning and
Brita Granström 1997

2TR(1FD)/0799/WKT/PW(PW)/140TMA

LIBRARY OF CONGRESS CATALOGING-IN-PUBLICATION DATA
Manning, Mick.
Nature Watch / Mick Manning, Brita Granström.
—1st American ed.
p.   cm.
Summary: Suggests ways to study nature, covering such areas as
field skills, tracks and droppings, animal homes, trees,
and rock pools.
1. Nature study—Activity programs—Juvenile literature.
[1. Nature study.]
I. Granström, Brita. II. Title.
QH54.5.M36 1997 508—dc20 96-30162 CIP AC

ISBN 0-7534-5063-1
Printed in Hong Kong

For Eric Sadler and John Norris Wood—my
own Nature Watch teachers.
—M.M.

NOTE: When you're out for a walk, take care to protect
yourself against deer ticks. Deer ticks carry a virus that causes illness,
including high fever. Cover your feet and legs entirely—with long pants, long
socks, and sturdy boots. Tuck pants into socks. Spray your feet and ankles
with tick repellent. Never spray directly onto your skin.
When you undress, check carefully for ticks. Check again
four days later; if you have a ringlike rash around a small
bite, see your doctor immediately.

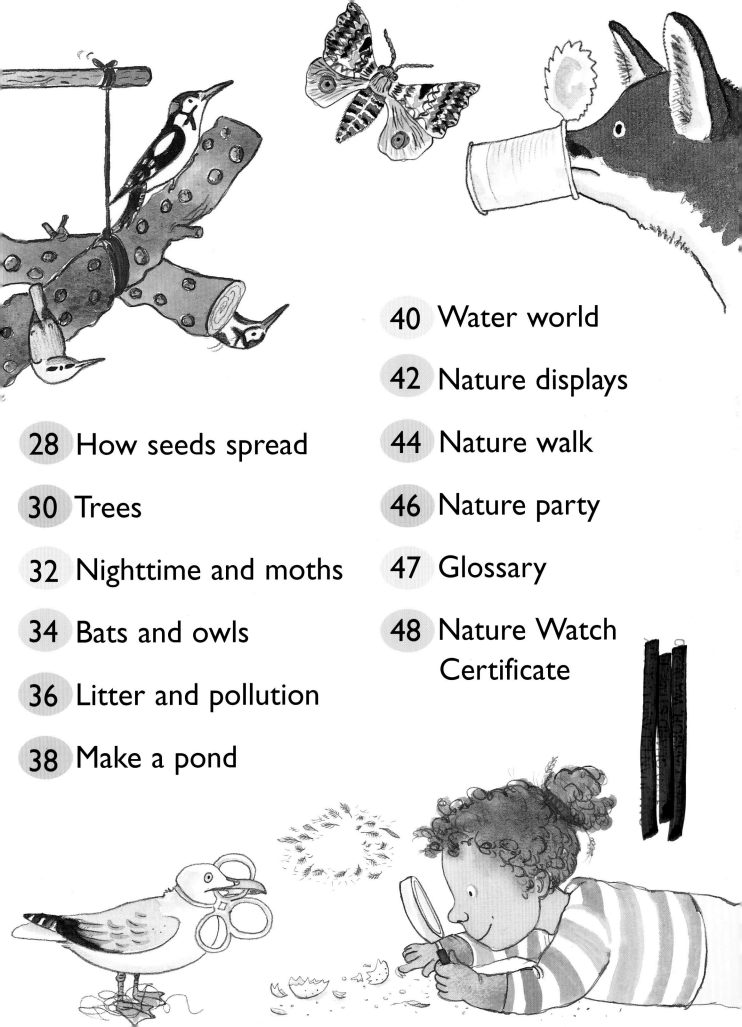

What this book is about!

Hi, I'm Mick ... Welcome to Nature Watch. Get ready to learn all about the world of nature!

Would you like to recognize different nature sounds and be able to name animal tracks? Would you like to feed hungry birds and keep wild animals safe? **Nature Watch** teaches you how to do all these things and a lot more besides. **Nature Watch** is full of exciting projects that will make you feel closer to the world around you.

Useful things

plastic bags

picnic lunc

daypack

gardening gloves

rubber gloves

waterproof coat and pants

binoculars

a flashlight

magnifying glass

tweezers

a good field guide

old clothes

old sneakers

pencil

notebook

colored pens

toilet paper or cotton balls

tape

whistle

NATURE TIPS

Helpful tips are in the colored strips on each page.

Throughout this book you will see words in **bold type**. Look in the glossary at the back of this book to find out more about these words.

Protect yourself against deer ticks! See page 2.

5

Wash any solid objects, such as shells, pebbles, and skulls, in disinfectant to kill any germs.

Always wash your hands and scrub under your nails after a nature hunt.

If you see sharp glass, syringes, or needles like this, don't touch them . . . tell a grown-up immediately.

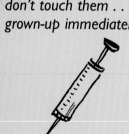

Never collect anything from dirty or polluted places and never wander off by yourself.

A nature notebook

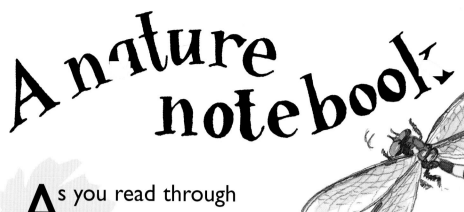

As you read through **Nature Watch**, keep a nature notebook—this should be a cross between a notepad, sketchbook, and scrapbook. Write down and draw all the things you see, and glue in photos and drawings. Take clippings from magazines and catalogs and put them in your notebook. Decorate the pages with some of your nature finds, such as leaves, seeds, petals, and feathers.

When you make drawings of the wildlife you see, write down details of the birds, animals, or objects you have seen, such as the color, sound, shape, and size, so that you can look them up in a guide if you need any more information later.

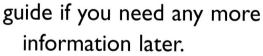

pine needle

Nature finds

Nature finds are things you find lying around, such as feathers, broken eggshells, bones, shells, and pebbles. You must never hurt or disturb animals or dig up plants.

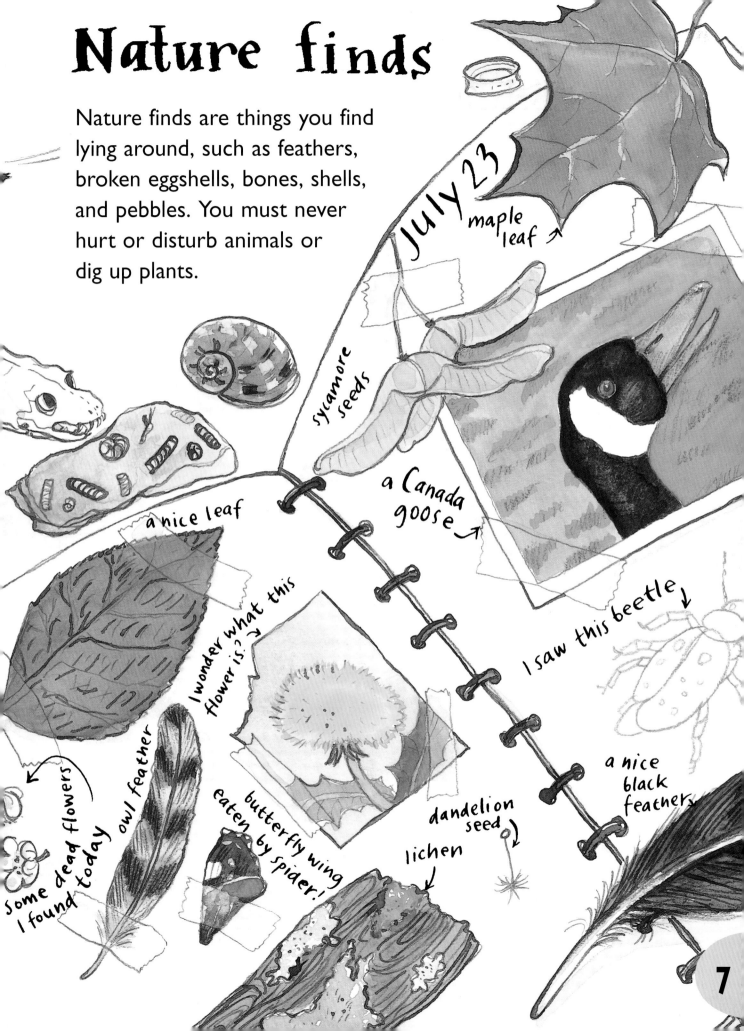

JULY 23

maple leaf →

sycamore seeds

a Canada goose ↘

a nice leaf

I wonder what this flower is? ↘

I saw this beetle ↓

a nice black feather

some dead flowers I found today

owl feather

butterfly wing eaten by spider!

dandelion seed ↘

lichen ↓

7

> You need to be very quiet

Wild animals are shy and secretive, so in order to see them you need to learn about field skills. Sometimes, to reach a good watching place without being seen, you may need to crawl across open ground as quietly as you can.

Try to be "downwind" of the animal you are watching. This means the wind is coming toward you and the animal will not be able to smell you. If the wind is going toward the animal, it will carry your smell with it.

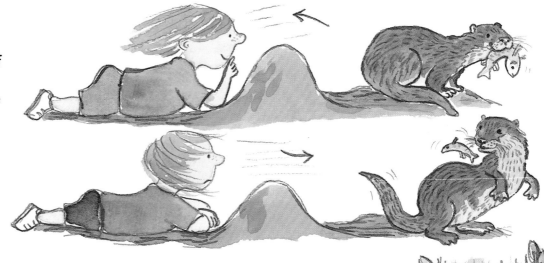

8

Most animals rely more on their smell and hearing than on their eyesight. So as long as you are downwind of the animal and stay silent, you shouldn't be spotted. Sit quietly with your back against a tree. Don't peep out from behind the tree when watching animals, since any sudden movement may scare them.

Make a hide you can wear

PROJECT

You will need: ● a sheer curtain or plastic mesh from a nursery ● green or brown dye ● scissors ● a bucket ● some leaves and grass.

If you use a sheer curtain, you need to dye it first. Mix the dye in a bucket—follow the instructions on the bottle. Soak the fabric in the dye. Dry the fabric and put it over your head. Mark where your face is. Cut out a hole for your face. Thread in some leaves and grass. Wear the "hide" over your head like a cape or a poncho.

Animal faces

PROJECT

Human faces often frighten wild animals. Try to disguise yourself using face paints. Make sure you use special non-toxic face paint. Do not use ordinary paint or you will hurt your skin. Try different disguises, such as a raccoon mask or a brown-faced weasel.

Nature detective

Be a detective and look for the signs that animals leave behind. Besides tracks and droppings, they leave behind many other clues. You can also look for their homes.

Clues to look for

Gnawed cherry stones and seeds mean mice or voles.

Watch for animal paths under fallen trees or bushes.

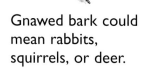

Gnawed bark could mean rabbits, squirrels, or deer.

Moth and butterfly wings mean a bat, bird, or spider has been feeding.

Hairs caught on a fence could be from sheep, rabbits, or foxes.

A fish skeleton may mean an otter or mink has had a tasty meal.

Circles or piles of feathers mean a kill by a predator. If the ends of the feathers are chewed, the predator was a mammal. If the feathers are plucked out, it was a bird of prey.

Flattened grass means an animal has been lying down.

0

Is anyone home?

PROJECT

Lay small sticks gently across the entrance of a burrow or animal hole. Any animal entering or leaving the hole will knock the sticks over as it passes. Go back and check the next day. Do not poke the sticks into the hole, as this might frighten or hurt the animal if it is at home.

NATURE TIPS

Tiny fish jumping around could mean a big hungry fish is chasing them.

Circles on the surface of a lake or river could mean that fish are eating insects.

Spot some animal homes!

PROJECT

A fox home, like the one in the tree below, is called a den or earth. You can tell if a fox is inside because the entrance will smell musky. Rabbits live in underground burrows or grass nests in fields, sandy banks, and under bushes. The ground around the entrance is often worn and covered with small round pellets or droppings. You will often find some rabbit fur near the holes, too.

A ball of leaves and twigs tucked in the corner of a branch and a tree trunk is a squirrel's home. A drilled hole in a tree usually means a woodpecker's nest. Dry mud around a hole is the work of a nuthatch. Sometimes other birds such as starlings steal a woodpecker hole. A bigger hole may be an owl's nest.

Tracks and droppings

You can learn a lot about animals by studying their tracks and droppings. Look for tracks by muddy paths and puddles, on sandy beaches, and in snow. If you find a dropping, try to guess whose it is.

Clues to look for

Droppings

Predator (fox)

Vegetarian (deer)

bird or lizard

mouse or vole

Tracks

fox dog cat

otter weasel mouse rat shrew

duck crow mini-beast squirrel horse deer sheep heron

a hopping rabbit or hare...

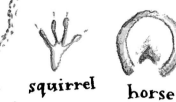

a leaping weasel...

a fox trotting and leaving a dropping

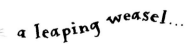

Have you had a mystery guest?

PROJECT

Nearly fill up a plastic bowl or other container with soft sand from a nursery. Smooth over the top.

On a plate put out something for your guests to eat, like dog biscuits, rabbit food, or cold oatmeal —lots of animals love cold oatmeal! Leave it overnight. Next day, look for tracks. Can you recognize the tracks left in the sand in the drawing?

NATURE TIPS

Don't touch droppings. If you want to examine them, poke them with a stick.

Keep a record in your nature notebook of tracks or droppings you find.

Small, white droppings were probably left by a bird or lizard.

Make a cast of tracks!

13

1

PROJECT

For two small casts you will need:
● a strip of cardboard 16 inches long and 2½ inches wide ● 2 paper clips ● plastic bowl or jug ● a quart bottle of water ● 2 large cups of plaster of paris ● stick for stirring ● bubble wrap or tissue paper.
1. Find a good, clear track in mud or sand, and carefully clear away any twigs or leaves.
2. Bend the strip into a circle to fit around your track, and join it together with the paper clips.
3. Using your stick, mix the plaster of paris with enough water to make it into a thick cream.
4. Pour it into your mold. When it is dry, after about twenty minutes, gently lift up the solid plaster of paris, keeping it in the cardboard strip. Carry it home carefully in bubble wrap or tissue paper.

When you get home, clean off the mud or soil with an old toothbrush. Use a marker pen to write on the cast the date and place you found the track, and the type of animal you think made it.

2

3

4

Wildlife feeding stations

Attract animals to your backyard or windowsill by putting out food. It is best to do this in the winter. Bread isn't really very good for birds—give them leftover food such as cereal, fat from meat, cheese, pasta, meaty bones, and potatoes. Avoid salty foods, and give them only fresh peanuts, never the roasted or salted kind.

Eating out

PROJECT

Make a simple windowsill feeder by wedging a sturdy stick across a window and hanging various feeders from it. Try making the recipes on the next page. Write down in your nature notebook which birds eat which foods.

Make peanut feeders from big plastic bottles. Cut a hole at the top on one side. Fill with fresh peanuts.

Make bird cake by mixing fresh peanuts and sunflower seeds with soft lard or shortening until the mixture is squishy. Thread string through the bottom of a yogurt container and fill it with the mixture.

Refrigerate the mixture until it is hard. Hang it upside down for bird acrobats.

For a log mobile, ask an adult to drill holes of different sizes into two small, dry logs. Stuff the holes with lard or fat. Tie the branches together in a cross shape. Hang the mobile outside at least 6 feet above the ground.

Bird apple pie

PROJECT

Take an old plastic bowl outside. Using your foot, squash up some old bruised apples. Spoon the apples into the bowl. Cover with a layer of uncooked oatmeal, fresh peanuts, and sunflower seeds. Put the bowl on your bird table. Watch who comes to eat from it.

Cut up fat from meat into small pieces for robins.

Potato surprise

PROJECT

Some birds are too shy to get to a window feeder or bird table, so here is a recipe especially for them. Stuff a baked potato with nuts, cheese, and seeds. Leave it in a quiet corner away from prowling cats. Who comes to eat it?

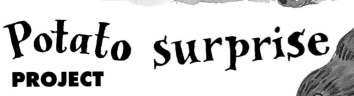

Put sunflower seeds in one of the feeders on your windowsill to attract finches.

Make a feeding station

Chickadees love pecking at peanuts in a net bag. Make sure the nuts are fresh, not salted or roasted.

15

PROJECT

It is easy to make a feeding station—ask a grown-up to nail an old tray to a wooden post like this. Make sure the table is high enough to be out of the reach of cats. Clear out old bits of food regularly.

Raccoons love dog biscuits, cold oatmeal, and raisins. If they do visit your yard, watch from a window so that you don't frighten them.

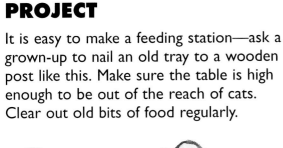

Animal homes

Once you have attracted animals to feed in your yard, why not make them some homes to live in? Then you can study them even more. Animal homes can be handmade by you, bought from a store, or just places that have become wild and overgrown.

Minibeast motel

PROJECT

Not all animals are cute and cuddly, but they are still interesting to watch. A melon makes a good motel for snails, slugs, pill bugs, bugs, and beetles. Halve a melon and eat the inside. Cut a door in one side with your spoon. Put the melon upside down in a damp corner out of the sun. Peek inside every morning to see how many guests are staying. It won't last long because the bugs will eat it, bit by bit.

MOTEL

Build a wild shelter
PROJECT

A pile of old branches, dead leaves, and hedge clippings near growing grass and tall weeds makes a good home for lizards, mice, and small, insect-eating birds. If you don't have a backyard, put some soil in a grow bag, then scatter grass and thistle seeds on top. Next, lay branches on top in a crisscross pattern. Make sure there are a lot of gaps to let in light and make room for your visitors. To study the animals, sit by the pile very quietly and watch who comes and goes.

NATURE TIPS

Always remember to keep your animal homes away from cats and dogs and other dangers.

Hang a bag of fresh peanuts or fat on your nesting box throughout the winter so the birds know the box is there.

Hang your box in a shady spot facing north to southeast.

17

Bird box
PROJECT

Ask a grown-up to make a bird nesting box for you—it's easy! Make one from plywood or other kinds of wood by following the plan on this page. Once you have cut out the pieces, carefully nail them together. Or you can buy a birdhouse from a nursery or a pet store.

8" — Side — 10"

10" — Side — 8"

8" — Front

Entrance hole 1¼" across

8½" — Roof

4½" — Base

drill small drain holes in base!

18" — Back

6"

Minibeasts

Small animals, such as insects, worms, and spiders, can be found everywhere—thousands can live in a small pile of dead leaves. They are **invertebrates** (animals without a backbone). To make it easier, some people refer to all of these small, spineless creatures as "minibeasts." When you try the following projects, make notes and drawings in your nature notebook about what different minibeasts look like.

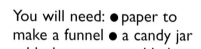

You will need: ● paper to make a funnel ● a candy jar ● black paper ● a table lamp ● cellophane tape ● damp tissue ● a magnifying glass ● gardening gloves

Minibeast funnel

PROJECT

Wrap the black paper around the jar and tape in place. Put a sheet of damp tissue in the bottom of the jar. Make a funnel out of paper and put it in the jar. Wearing gloves, take a handful of dead leaves and put them in the funnel. Shine your light on top of the leaves (not too close) and leave it for an hour. When you come back, some of the tiny minibeasts will have dropped into the jar. Look closely at them, using a magnifying glass. Draw how they look in your nature notebook.

18

We are all minibeasts!

Check a plant

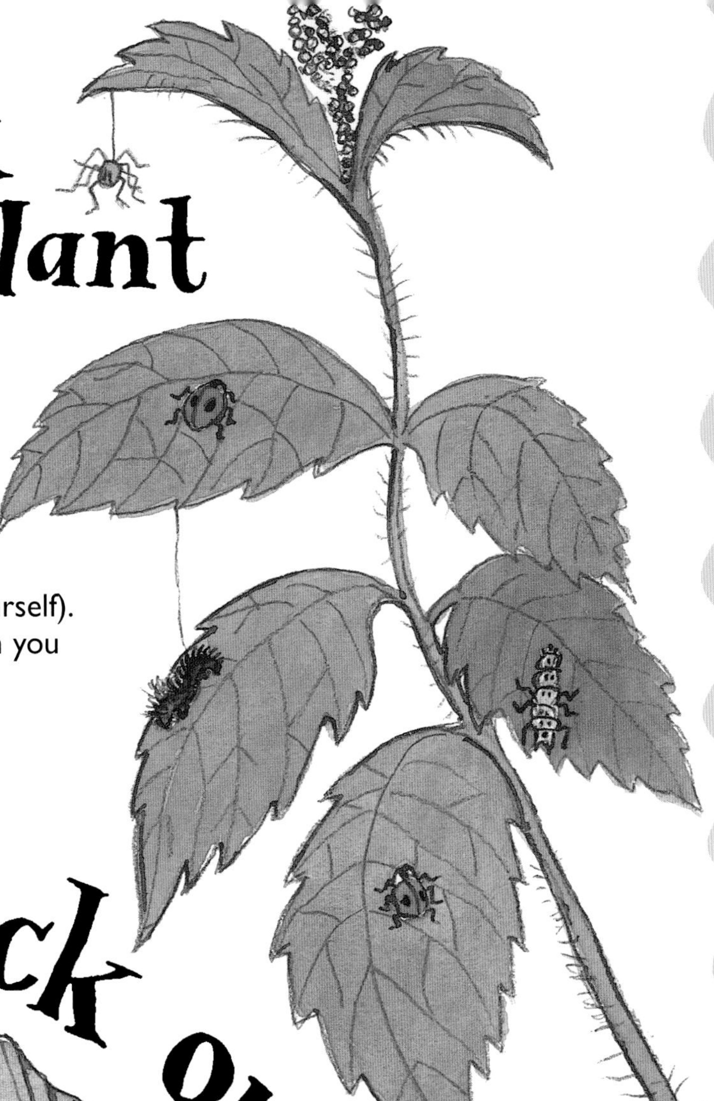

PROJECT

One healthy plant can be home to lots of different kinds of minibeasts. Find a plant, such as a nettle or a rosebush (be careful not to scratch yourself). How many minibeasts can you see living on this plant?

NATURE TIPS

A magnifying glass is useful for looking at minibeasts.

Always wear gloves when picking up leaves or studying plants.

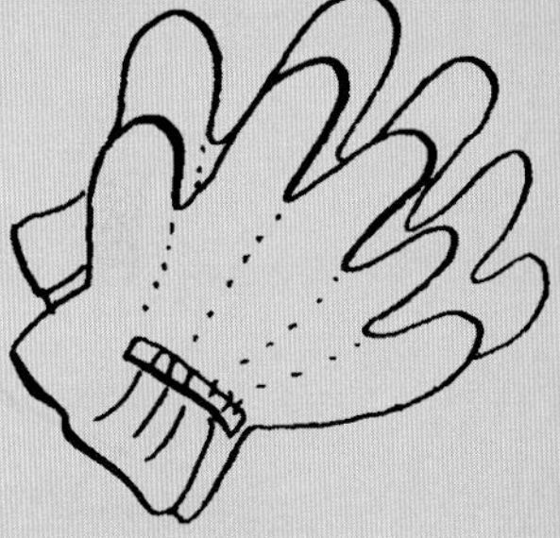

Check out a rotten log

harvestman
wood beetle
beetle grub
millipede
centipede
weevil
pill bug
rove beetle

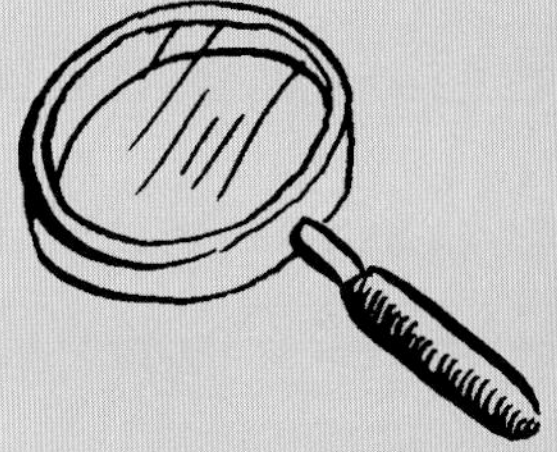

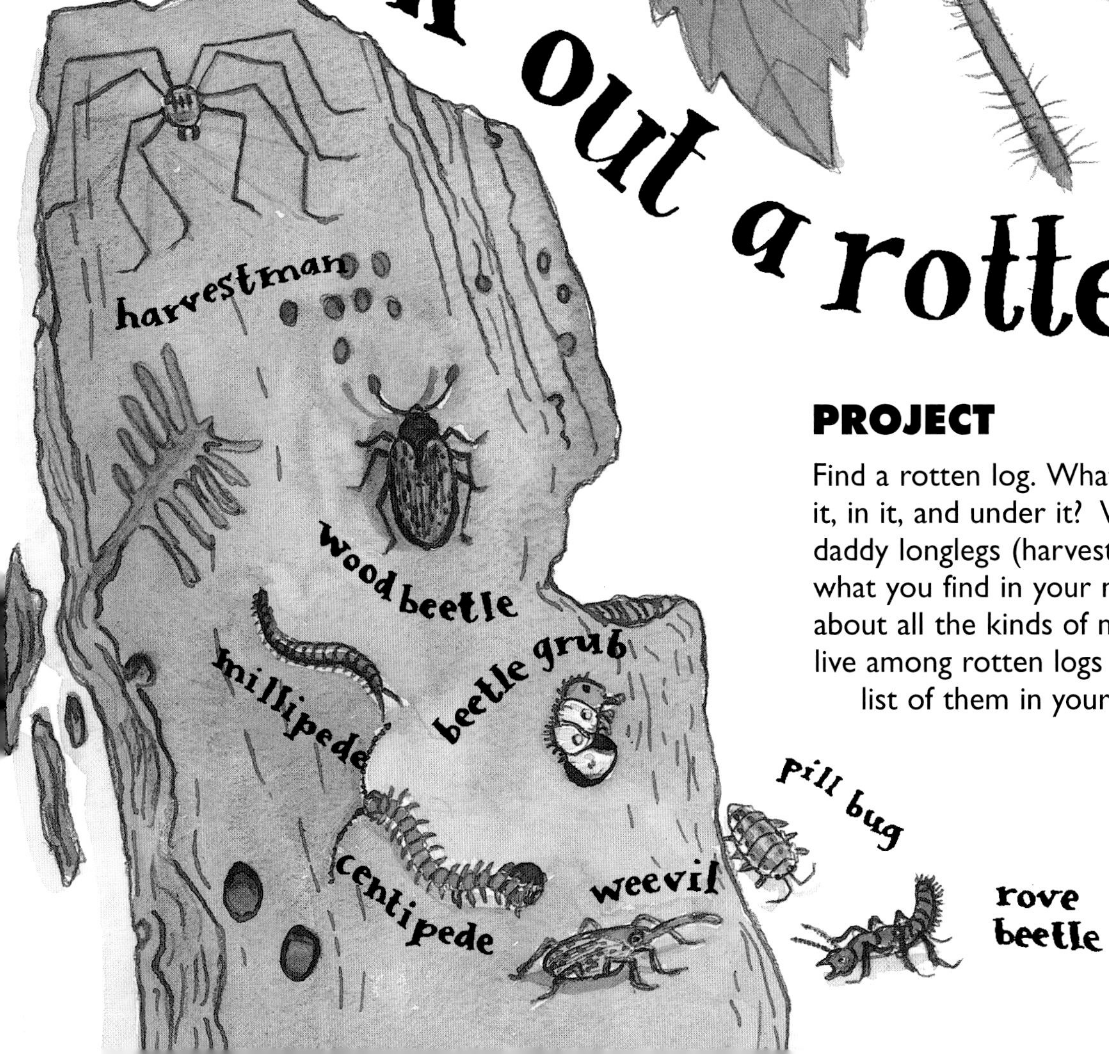

PROJECT

Find a rotten log. What can you see living on it, in it, and under it? Worms, beetles, and a daddy longlegs (harvestman) perhaps? Draw what you find in your nature notebook. Think about all the kinds of minibeasts that might live among rotten logs and leaves—write a list of them in your nature notebook.

Fungi

Some kinds of fungi (including many mushrooms and toadstools) are very poisonous, so never eat any fungi you find, and always wear gloves when touching them. Now you can have fun collecting all the different kinds of fungi. In your nature notebook, draw the patterns you see on the underside of their caps.

Spore prints

PROJECT

Fungi scatter a dustlike powder, called spores, which will grow into new fungi. Lay some edible mushroom caps on squares of paper and leave them overnight. Next day, carefully lift them up and you will see that they have left patterns of spores on the paper. To keep the spore dust from flying off the paper or smudging, spray it very gently with hairspray. Do not hold the hairspray too close to the paper. Glue the patterns in your nature notebook or hang them on a wall in your home.

20

Spot different shapes

Next time you go on a nature walk, see how many different fungus shapes you can find.

Growing mold

PROJECT

Mold is a small kind of fungus that grows from tiny spores that float in the air all around us. Take an old bruised apple or a piece of bread and put it in a jar. Make air holes in the lid before putting it on. Soon mold will begin to grow. Watch your mold grow and develop until it covers all of the fruit. Once this has happened, throw the jar away.

NATURE TIPS

Wear gloves when touching fungi, and always wash your hands afterward.

Grow mold from food, such as cheese, fruit, and bread. See how different each mold looks.

When you have grown your mold in a jar, paint it in your nature notebook. Use colored pencils or watercolors.

Worm farm

Worms are very helpful. They eat dead leaves and aerate the soil with their tunnels. They help fertilize the soil, too. Worms are both male and female in one body. Animals like this are called hermaphrodites.

Make a worm farm

PROJECT

You will need: ● a plastic bottle ● a large glass or plastic jar ● soil and sand ● a rubber band ● black paper ● cellophane tape ● leaves and grass ● panty hose or other mesh material for the lid. Cut the bottom off the plastic bottle and put the bottle in the large jar. Pour layers of soil and sand in the space between the bottle and the jar and dampen it. Collect some worms and put them on top of the soil and sand. Put some leaves and grass on top for the worms to eat. Stretch the mesh material over the top of the jar to make a lid. Wrap black paper around the jar, and hold it in place with tape. Leave the jar in a cool place for two days. When you take off the paper, you will see the worms' tunnels. Let the worms go after a week, or they may die.

22

cut a plastic bottle

sand and soil

a large jar

leaves for food

mesh for lid

black paper

rubber band

Dances with Worms!

Birds attract worms to the surface of the ground by stamping on it. See if you can do this by trying this special worm dance. Gently stamp your feet and move around on a patch of earth or grass. After about five minutes stop and see if any worms have come to the surface. Write down in your nature notebook how many worms have appeared.

NATURE TIPS

Look for worm casts. Worms squeeze out undigested soil from their bodies like toothpaste out of a tube.

When digging for worms, don't use a shovel, as this may hurt them. Use a small garden fork to lift the soil gently. Or pour a bucket of water slowly onto a patch of grass and worms might crawl to the surface.

23

Listen to the Worms

PROJECT

Put a worm or two on a sheet of paper. Put your ear close to the paper and listen. Can you hear the worms' bristles scratching as they crawl along? The bristles help the worms get a grip. Remember to put the worms back where you found them.

Changing bodies

Metamorphosis is the name for the way some animals change their shape completely as they grow, like a caterpillar turning into a butterfly or a grub into a ladybug. Butterflies have very delicate wings with tiny scales on them, like dust, so try not to touch them with your fingers.

caterpillars

Butterflies are insects that fly by day and have brightly colored wings. They like to feed on flowers and sunbathe in warm places. A butterfly starts life as an egg, which hatches into a caterpillar. The caterpillar feeds on plants and later turns into a chrysalis. The butterfly forms inside the chrysalis.

24

egg

caterpillar

chrysalis

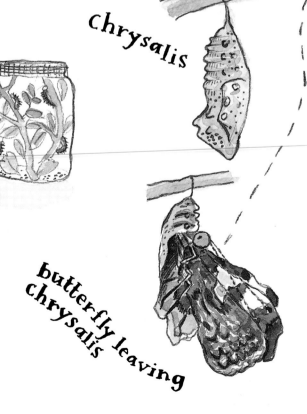

butterfly leaving chrysalis

PROJECT

Look around wild plants and cabbage patches to find some common caterpillars. Put them in a box or jar with leaves from the plant you found them on. Put a net lid on the jar, such as fine mesh panty hose, so that they get plenty of light and fresh air—use cellophane tape or a rubber band to hold the lid in place. Every day, take out the old leaves and put in fresh leaves for them to eat and twigs to crawl on. As the caterpillars grow and change, draw the different stages of their metamorphosis in your nature notebook. When the caterpillars turn into chrysalises, be patient and do not touch them. When the butterflies hatch, let them dry their wings and then, very gently, let them go.

NATURE TIPS

Make a tall home for your caterpillars by cutting the top off one plastic bottle and the top and bottom off another. Join the two plastic bottles together with cellophane tape. Cover the top with fine mesh, and hold in place with more tape.

25

Grow plants for butterflies

PROJECT

To attract butterflies, plant buddleia and wild asters in your backyard, and catnip and marjoram in a window box.

Look at ladybugs

ladybug

eggs

pupa

grub

Ladybugs also go through several different stages. The adult ladybug lays eggs which turn into grubs, then pupae, then more adults.

You can keep ladybugs, too! But they are predators and have to have a fresh supply of leaves with aphids and plant bugs to eat every day.

Nuts, beans, cones, and seeds

Nuts and seeds grow into new plants and trees. Beans and seeds come in all shapes and sizes. You can get them from stores or look for them on your nature walks.

String beans

PROJECT

Line a glass jar with damp blotting paper and fill it with soil, newspaper, or cotton balls to hold the blotting paper tight against the jar. Push some string beans, lima beans, or sunflower seeds between the jar and the blotting paper. Put the jar in a warm, dark place until the beans and seeds begin to sprout. Check the jar every day. Draw the changes in your nature notebook.

Farm your own crop

PROJECT

This is a kind of farming—growing plants for food. You will need: ● a saucer ● cotton balls or blotting paper ● mung beans from a health food store

26

1. Put some wet cotton balls or blotting paper on a saucer or in a jar. **2.** Put the saucer in a warm place, and make sure you keep the cotton balls or blotting paper wet by spraying with water. **3.** Soon the beans will sprout and begin to grow. **4.** After two or three days, the beans should be big enough for you to cut and add to a salad. So now you can say you are a farmer! Try growing other beans for sandwiches and salads.

Plant a nut

PROJECT

Next time you go on a nature walk, pick up some acorns, chestnuts, and other nuts. Soak some of them in a bowl overnight. The next day, plant each nut in a separate pot. Label it with a popsicle stick. Leave some indoors and put some outdoors over the winter. If you are lucky, by the spring tiny oak or chestnut trees may have begun to grow. In your nature notebook, write down which nuts grew first, the indoor or the outdoor ones. Keep a record of how quickly they grow.

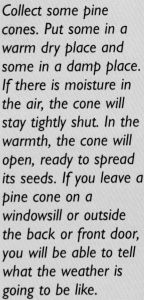

27

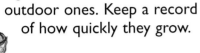

Cone prints

On your next nature walk, pick up some cones. Cones carry the seeds of conifer trees and have woody scales to protect their small seeds from damage. In warm weather they open up, and the seeds flutter away on the breeze, hopefully to grow into new conifers. Most cones stay on the tree for a year before their seeds are ready. To make cone prints, roll out some colored modeling clay and press different kinds of cones into it. Keep a note of the patterns and which tree each cone came from.

How seeds spread

Seeds are spread in a lot of different ways—some stick to fur and sweaters, some float in the air, some fly like helicopter blades, others are spread through animal droppings. How many seeds can you find and record in your nature notebook? Berries are cases for seeds—they are soft fruits with lots of little seeds inside. Some berries are very poisonous, so never eat any wild berries that you find.

Berries for birds

The seeds of berries such as raspberries and blackberries are spread by birds and animals who eat the ripe fruit and then deposit the seeds in their droppings. Collect some berries, put them out for the birds, and note down who eats what.

Plants from your shoes

You can spread seeds, too! To prove it, grow some plants from your shoes. After a nature walk, scrape the mud from your shoes into a plant pot. Water it. Put it outdoors and watch it grow. Do you recognize any of the plants?

Make a fruit Salad

PROJECT

Most fruit has seeds inside. Some seeds you can eat, some you can't. Buy a few of your favorite fruits. Cut them in half. Quickly sketch the patterns the seeds make. Later on, you can draw them in your nature notebook and color them in. Slice the fruit. Put to one side the seeds you can't eat, and save them for the next project. Put the fruit pieces into a bowl. Add some fruit juice and a little sugar to taste. Mix the fruit together and serve with ice cream, or just by itself.

Make a sycamore nose like this...

Plant the Seeds

PROJECT

Plant some of the fruit seeds in yogurt containers or plant pots. Make small holes in the bottom of the containers for drainage. Fasten a plastic bag over the top of the pot with a rubber band. Bend a straw into the bag. Blow into it to fill the bag with air. You now have a mini greenhouse for your fruit to grow in. Label the pots. Remember to take the bag off once the seeds start sprouting.

Trees

Trees can grow to be among the biggest things on earth! A tree is a plant, and like all plants it uses sunlight to make food and to grow. Trees help us by making oxygen for us to breathe and by absorbing poisonous gases like carbon dioxide. Trees can live for many hundreds of years. To find out how old a tree is, measure around the trunk. Every inch stands for about one year in the tree's life.

Hugging a tree

PROJECT

Hug a tree! Close your eyes and feel the texture of the bark. Smell the trunk. Listen to the sounds around the tree—insects buzzing and birds singing. Hug five different trees and write down the feel, smell, and noise of each in your nature notebook. Collect some leaves that have fallen off the tree and make a bark rubbing (see page 31). Put these things together in your notebook. Now you have a complete picture of each tree.

Bark rubbings

PROJECT

Make bark rubbings to go with your pressed leaves and nature notes. Use sheets of plain paper and a big crayon to get the best results. Rub gently and don't damage the tree trunk. When you get home, try washing over the rubbing with watery paint—this will make it even clearer. Remember to note the tree it came from and where you did the bark rubbing.

Red celery

PROJECT

Mix some red ink with water in a jar or vase. Stand a stick of celery in it and watch what happens over the next day or two. The leaves should turn pink—this shows how water is carried around a tree. A tree can have as much as 25 gallons of water moving around inside it.

Pressed leaves

PROJECT

To press leaves for your nature notebook, place the leaves between sheets of blotting paper. Press them between two heavy books—you could add a brick for extra weight!

*Nighttime animals are called **nocturnal**.*

Moths are night-flying insects that look like butterflies but tend to have duller colored wings. If you keep any moths to study, always let them go at night, not during the day.

32

Nighttime
and moths

As the sun goes down, listen carefully to what you can hear. Frogs may be calling, crickets may be chirping, birds may be singing. We call this time of day dusk.

PROJECT

Listen to the night noises. Write down who you think is making each noise. Make sound patterns on a sheet of paper. Use a different color for each sound. When you have finished, you will have composed a sheet of night music. Listen for the birds singing early in the morning, too. This is sometimes called the dawn chorus. Compose a sheet of dawn chorus music, too!

Sugaring

PROJECT

Mix together some concentrated fruit juice with a pint of hot water. Then dissolve two tablespoons of corn syrup or molasses and four tablespoons of sugar in it. Paint the mixture on a fence or tree trunk. Even better, soak a bunch of rags in it and hang them up. In the evening, check to see if moths come and feed.

Hang up a sheet

PROJECT

Another good way to spot moths and other nighttime insects is to hang a white sheet on a clothesline or a tree. When it gets dark, shine a spotlight or a flashlight onto it. Soon, moths will come and land on the sheet. Have a good look at them. See if they are different from ones you've seen before.

Moths are night-flying insects...

Bats and Owls

Bats are brilliant nighttime hunters. They eat hundreds of insects every night. They live in old buildings, caves, hollow trees, and roof spaces. Owls are beautiful, mysterious birds. Most owls are **nocturnal** (active at night), but some can be **diurnal** (active during the day).

Bat ears

PROJECT

Bats are not blind, but they hunt in the dark using *echolocation*—this means that they listen to the echo of their own squeaks bouncing off objects in the dark. This is how they can "see" well enough in the dark to catch insects and not to crash into things. Make two paper funnels like the one in the drawing. Hold one to each ear—you will soon understand why a bat's ears are so big.

34

How to make an owl hoot

Clasp your hands together like this.

PROJECT

Talk to owls by making hooting noises with your hands. Hoot out of your window at night —you never know, occasionally an owl may hoot back!

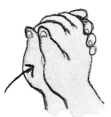

Bend your thumbs slightly to make a hole. Blow into the hole.

Hide and squeak!

PROJECT

Copy the mouse and owl drawings shown above onto a sheet of thin cardboard and color them. Make a hole on either side of each mask. Thread a length of elastic, long enough to fit around your head, through the holes and knot the ends. Cut eye holes so that you can see clearly. You need only one owl mask, but make plenty of mice masks. Try adding fishing line "whiskers" on the mice! Then invite your friends over to play "hide and squeak!" One of you has to be the owl. The others are the mice. The mice go and hide and make squeaking noises. The owl tries to find them. The last mouse to be found becomes the owl for the next game.

Owl pellets

Owls are birds of prey. They feed on small mammals and birds, and then they make pellets. Pellets are small balls of fur and bones coughed up after a meal. You can find pellets wherever owls sleep, perch, and nest.

Here are things you might find...

PROJECT

Look for owl pellets under trees, fences, and poles. Put a pellet in an old tin can or mug, and pour some warm water and a little disinfectant over it. Let it soak for ten minutes. Pour out the water and put the pellet on a sheet of paper. Gently pull it apart with two old forks or a pair of tweezers.

Litter and Pollution

Litter can hurt wild animals—even trash thrown away in a bag can be dangerous to wildlife if the bag is torn open. To be absolutely safe and to help the environment, **recycle** as much trash as you can. Take old bottles and newspapers to special **recycling units**—if you don't know where your nearest units are, ask your city hall. If you have a garden, start a compost heap with waste scraps of food such as vegetable peelings, eggshells, and used teabags.

Bottles

Thrown-away bottles become death traps for insects and other small animals. They crawl inside and slip down the neck of the bottle. Once inside, they are trapped. If you find a thrown-away bottle, block up the neck with paper and insert a stick—this will stop animals from crawling in and help minibeasts to crawl out! If you can, put the bottle in a bag and throw it in a bin. Never pick up broken bottles.

Tin Cans

Scavenging animals and birds can get tin cans stuck on their noses or beaks when they poke around garbage cans and garbage dumps. To stop this from happening, squash all cans before you throw them away. Carefully tuck the lid into the can and squash it by stamping on it. What would you do if you were a fox with a tin can stuck on your nose? Write a story in your notebook about how you would get it off.

Other dangers...

Plastic rings that hold cans of beer and soft drinks together can get stuck around the necks of animals. Always cut the rings with scissors before you throw them away. Nylon string or old fishing line can get tangled around the legs or necks of animals and birds. Cut them into short pieces before throwing away, and never leave fishing line lying around. Always throw litter away.

Oil pollution

Sometimes, large amounts of oil are poured into the seas by ships that have been wrecked, or when there has been an accident on an oil rig. When this happens, seals and sea birds get oil clogged in their fur or feathers, and they can drown or swallow poisonous oil. Imagine that you are a bird that has swum into a patch of oil. What does it feel like? What would you do next? Write the story in your nature notebook.

NATURE TIPS

If you find an injured creature, gently cover it with a coat or towel before asking an adult to pick it up. Keep your face away from it (be particularly careful of sharp beaks). Keep quiet around it and don't make sudden movements. Always phone a wildlife rescue service (keep the number in your notebook). A cardboard box is a safe, dark place to keep a creature until help arrives.

Acid rain

A serious kind of **pollution** is caused by chemicals from factories and chimneys, which go into the sky as dirty smoke and fall back to Earth as acid rain. These projects show what acid rain can do.

PROJECT

Put some vinegar in a glass or jar and drop in a piece of white chalk. Watch what happens. This is how acid rain dissolves stonework in buildings, although it happens much more slowly than your experiment.

PROJECT

Pick some leaves with their stalks. Stand them in a cup or jar of vinegar for a few days. Write down what happens in your nature notebook. This is a speeded-up version of what acid rain does to trees.

Keep a list of any pollution you find near your home, whatever it is. Can you see any signs of acid rain pollution, like brown patches on leaves or dead branches, or partly dissolved statues or stones?

Remember to keep your pond topped up in hot weather so that animals are able to crawl in and out easily. Put in a log bridge to help them.

If you have younger brothers or sisters, ask a grown-up to cover your pond with chicken wire or a fence to keep them from falling in.

Make a pond

Ponds are important for all sorts of wildlife, both as homes and as places to come and drink. You don't need a big yard to have a pond—you can even make a pond in a jelly jar!

Pond in a bowl

1.

Make your very own pond. You can make it in an old plastic bowl, a bucket, or even an old sink.

2.

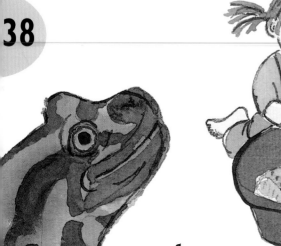

38

You will need: ● a plastic bowl ● big and small stones ● pond weed from a nursery ● some soil or sand.

1. Take the plastic bowl and dig it into the soil or place it in a quiet corner in your yard. Cover the bottom with sand. Put in some small stones and a couple of bigger stones that will poke above the surface of the water.

2. Put in some pond weed to keep the water fresh. Tie clumps of the pond weed to the stones to keep it on the bottom.

3.

3. Once you have prepared it, carefully fill your pond to the brim with clear water. Pile stones and old logs around the edge as a shelter for bugs and **amphibians**. After a few weeks all sorts of tiny creatures and plants will begin to live there. Birds will drink and bathe in it, and perhaps frogs, newts, and colorful dragonflies will come to visit or stay. Keep notes and drawings in your notebook of the interesting things that happen in your pond in a bowl. Don't take any frogs or newts from the wild because they may already have somewhere to live. But they might come to you. Make them a little ramp to help them climb in and out of the pond.

Pond in a jar!

PROJECT

If you don't have space for a pond in a bowl, you can make a smaller pond in a jar. Fill a clean jar with tiny stones, weeds, and water, and leave it on your windowsill for a few weeks. All sorts of tiny creatures like water fleas and **algae** will come and live there. If you fill your jar with water from an existing pond, the number of creatures in your jar will be even greater.

Water world

If you visit the beach, see if you can find a tide pool. The creatures who live in tide pools have their homes filled up twice a day when the tide comes in.

Make an underwater viewer

PROJECT

Reflections on the surface of the water can make it difficult to see into the pool. You can make an underwater viewer to see better. You will need: ● a plastic bottle ● plastic bag or plastic wrap ● waterproof tape ● scissors ● a pen. Cut off the bottom of the bottle. Stretch the plastic wrap across the bottom of the bottle and tape it in place. Push it below the surface of the tide pool and peep through the top. Sit quietly and see what animals you can spot. Look for small fish and shrimp hiding in the seaweed. Never take plants or creatures out of the tide pool. Do you know the names of the creatures in this tide pool?

See inside a shell

The empty shells you find on the beach are the old homes of shellfish. These shells can be wonderful shapes. Look closely and you will see rings like the lines on a tree trunk, made as the shellfish grew. Hold a shell to your ear—can you hear the sea? Rub an empty shell against a sheet of sandpaper. Slowly you will rub away one side of the shell and be able to see inside. Draw the different shapes you find.

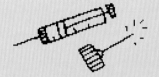
What can you find on the beach?

shells

feather

bird skull

razor shell

crab claw

egg case

seaweed holding a pebble

seaweed

hell

crab

pebble

Nature displays

All through this book you have been collecting your nature finds. Why not put them on display for your family and friends to see? Here are some suggestions . . . .

Feathers

You can find dropped feathers almost anywhere. Small ones come from the bird's body and large ones come from the wings. Display them by gluing them onto pieces of styrofoam or modeling clay. Label them with the name of the bird you think they have come from.

Fossils

Fossils are the remains of animals that lived millions of years ago, which have become pressed together with sand or mud and have become stone. You can find rocks with fossils in them at the beach, near the river, or even in your backyard. Look for patterns in pebbles like the one drawn here. Smooth pebbles or shiny crystals would look nice in your collection,

Storage

If you don't want to put your finds on display right away, make sure you store them carefully once you have cleaned and labeled them. Pack them in a shoe box or an old cake tin filled with tissue paper. For small finds, use empty matchboxes or small candy boxes.

Make a display box

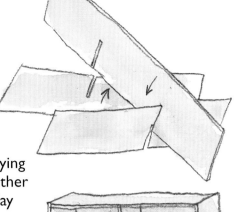

PROJECT

Cardboard boxes are good for displaying your finds. Ask at supermarkets or other stores for empty boxes. Make a display case like this: measure the inside edges of a cardboard box. Cut cardboard strips to fit. Make slits to fit the strips together. Slot them together to make shelves and put them in your box. Tiny display boxes can be made from the inside of a large matchbox with plastic wrap stretched across the front and taped to the back of the box.

Clean up a skull

If you find an animal or bird skull, scrub it clean with an old toothbrush and water with disinfectant added to it. Then leave it outside so that the sun can bleach it white naturally. Always wear rubber gloves when cleaning your finds and wash your hands and scrub under your nails afterward so that you don't catch any germs.

Find out more

Find out more about nature. Visit your local library and look up the birds, animals, minibeasts, or other objects you have found. Make notes about them your nature notebook. You can also read about the birds and other creatures that live in different parts of the world. Find out if there is a young naturalists club in your area or a bird-watching group you can join.

Nature walk

Do you enjoy listening to birds singing in spring, or hearing the wind blowing through the trees in the fall? Would you like to see animals in the wild? If the answers are yes, then you have started to develop your feelings for nature. So put on a pair of sturdy boots, grab your notebook, and let's go for a walk. Nature walks are also an ideal opportunity to find things for your nature displays.

44

Listen to nature

Choose a quiet place. It could be in your backyard or garden, in a park, or in the countryside, depending on where you live. Sit quietly and write down all the sounds you can hear. Try to describe each sound in words like "trickling water," "rustling leaves," "buzzing insects," or "squeaking animals."

Smell nature

Choose three different natural things, such as a flower, a stone, and a leafy branch. Take a good sniff of each one! Try to write down a description of the smells in your nature notebook.

45

Look closer!

Choose somewhere that you can get to easily and safely and that you know and like. Now get down on all fours and have a really close look at the hidden details of nature on the ground. Amazing, isn't it!

NATURE TIPS

Have a nature quiz. Write out ten questions, such as "Guess how many acorns there are in this jar?" or "Whose feather is this?" Give the answers at the end of the quiz, and a nature prize to the winner.

46

Nature party

At the end of your nature watch have a nature party! Invite your friends and parents to read your nature notebook and look at your collections and displays. Ask everyone to come dressed as their favorite animal, insect, or plant. Play nature music and make some nature party food—salad with bean sprouts, fruit, and bread and honey. Have fun!

Glossary

Aerate
To let air into soil, to help keep it healthy.

Algae
Tiny plants that grow in fresh or saltwater or on moist ground.

Amphibians
Cold-blooded creatures with a backbone that live on land but breed in water. Frogs, toads, and newts are all amphibians.

Carbon dioxide
A gas in the air that can be poisonous to animals if there is too much of it.

Compost heap
A way of recycling kitchen and garden waste and using it to make fertilizer for your

garden. It also makes a good home for animals.

Conifer
A tree or a shrub that bears cones and has evergreen leaves shaped like needles.

Diurnal
A word used to describe a bird or animal that is active only during the day.

Environment
A word used to describe the world we live in.

Invertebrates
Animals without a backbone. Minibeasts, such as spiders and worms, are invertebrates.

Nocturnal
A word used to describe a bird or animal that is active only at nighttime.

Oxygen
An invisible gas in the air that all animals need to breathe to stay alive.

Pollution
A word used to describe threats to our environment made by human waste products and litter.

Predator
An animal that kills and eats other animals.

Recycle
To use things like glass, paper, and aluminum more than once.

Recycling units
Places where glass, cans, and paper are made into new things.

Vegetarian
An animal that eats only plants.

47

Nature
WATCH
Certificate

Name _____

has completed the

Nature
WATCH

with excellence

Date _____   Age _____

Mick Manning—Teacher

Mick Manning.